UNVEILING DUAL LIVES

THE MAKING OF

SEVERANCE

A FAN'S IN-DEPTH ANALYSIS OF SEASON ONE AND TWO

MICHAEL S. SAGE

The Making of Severance

Unveiling Dual Lives - A Fan's In-depth Analysis of Season One and Two

By

Michael S. Sage

Disclaimer

This book is an independent publication and is not authorized, sponsored, or endorsed by the creators, cast, or producers of *Severance* or any associated entities. The content within is based on the author's personal analysis, research, and interpretations of the series.

All trademarks, titles, and characters related to *Severance* are the property of their respective owners. This book is intended for informational and entertainment purposes only, offering a fan's perspective on the show's themes, production, and cultural impact.

Limitation of Liability

The content provided in this book is for informational and entertainment purposes only. While every effort has been made to ensure the accuracy of the information presented, the author and publisher make no representations or warranties of any kind, express or implied, about the completeness, accuracy, reliability, or suitability of the content.

By using this book, readers acknowledge and agree that the author and publisher shall not be held liable for any direct, indirect, incidental, consequential, or punitive damages arising out of the use of this book, including but not limited to errors or omissions in the content.

This book is a fan-created work, and any opinions or interpretations expressed are solely those of the author. Readers are encouraged to verify any details independently if necessary.

Gratitude

I want to take a moment to express my deepest appreciation to everyone who has supported this journey. To the creators, cast, and crew of *Severance*, your brilliance inspired every word within these pages. To the readers, your curiosity and passion for unraveling the mysteries of this series fuel the dedication behind this work.

To my friends, family, and colleagues, thank you for your encouragement and belief in this endeavor. And to the fans of *Severance*—thank you for sharing this collective fascination with a story that challenges our perspectives on identity, duality, and the human condition. This book is a labor of love, born from the shared admiration for storytelling that dares to be bold. Thank you for being part of this journey. Your support makes it all worthwhile.

Table of Contents

INTRODUCTION

An Overview of the Severance World

The Idea That Underlies the Show

Severance is fundamentally an eerie examination of identity, free will, and the delicate balancing act between personal and professional commitments. The series provides a terrifyingly bizarre look at the corporate world via the prism of science fiction. It was created by Dan Erickson and was brought to life by Ben Stiller and Aoife McArdle. Lumon Industries, a biotechnological company that invented the contentious "severance" process, is the focus of the narrative. Employees' consciousness is surgically split into two distinct entities by this process: their *"Innie"* self, who only exists within the boundaries of their workplace, and their *"Outie"* self, who lives outside of it.

In addition to being intriguing, this notion is extremely unnerving. *Severance* explores the moral conundrums of autonomy and exploitation by separating work from home life. The Innies are doomed to a never-ending workday, their existence a monotonous routine of chores with no escape or personal significance. On the other hand, outies do not have to worry about their jobs, but they do have to give up a large part of their lives. The contradiction poses important queries, such as: Is it really possible to compartmentalize identity without repercussions? Who is morally qualified to split someone's life in two?

Severance's genius resides in its ability to blend profoundly personal stories with high-concept science fiction. The show tells a story of corporate tyranny, individual pain, and defiance against a system that feeds on dehumanization through its protagonist, Mark Scout (Adam Scott), and a cast of well-developed characters.

Inspirations and Creative Genesis

Dan Erickson's life experiences and artistic goals served as the foundation for *Severance*. Erickson was working a boring office job and longed to get away from the monotony of the 9–5 grind. This desire sowed the seeds for the central idea of the series. He wondered, "What if you could avoid the parts of life you didn't want to go through?" The concept struck a chord with universal issues of contemporary work-life balance, but Erickson went one step further by conceiving of a scenario in which that escape came at an unimaginable price.

Erickson was able to create *Severance's* intricate plot thanks to his experience writing plays and his degree in television writing at NYU. He added intimacy and genuineness to the play by drawing on his relationships with his siblings and his own thoughts on identity and memory. According to Erickson, several of the series' characters were modeled off his own family dynamics, which gives the otherwise fantastical plot a more relatable touch.

Severance's script originally attracted notice when it was included in the 2016 Blood List, which is a list of the genre's greatest unproduced screenplays. Known for his versatility as a director and performer, Ben Stiller found the script through Red Hour Productions, his production firm. Stiller saw the potential of Erickson's idea right away, characterizing the pilot as the ideal fusion of psychological suspense and workplace humor.

Erickson and Stiller's joint efforts served as the cornerstone of *Severance's* prosperity. The series' careful pace and atmospheric tension are clear examples of Stiller's directing impact. Even though Stiller had only intended to direct the pilot, he became very involved with the project and ended up directing six of the nine episodes in the first season. *Severance* became a genre-defining series because of his meticulous attention to detail and dedication to the emotional depth of the narrative.

Creating Lumon's World

Another noteworthy feature of *Severance* is its world-building, which combines apocalyptic overtones with vintage aesthetics. The architectural designs of modernist luminaries such as Eero Saarinen served as a source of inspiration for production designer Jeremy Hindle. Filmed in the Bell Labs Holmdel Complex in New Jersey, Lumon Industries' offices have a timeless yet confusing feel. Its expansive passageways and simple design reflect the psychological state of the fired employees by fostering a sense of power and seclusion.

Viewers are further drawn into the bizarre setting by the props and set elements. For the performers, old computers were recreated with practical duties that replicated the boredom of actual office work. As a metaphor for the Innies' imprisoned existence, these machines lacked an escape key. The series' thematic richness is highlighted by this attention to detail, where each design element has a narrative function.

Severance's temporal uncertainty is yet another brilliant move. The show confuses viewers by fusing automobiles, technology, and fashion from several eras, causing Lumon Industries to feel disconnected from any particular period or location. This imaginative decision heightens the spooky ambiance and creates a sense of familiarity and alienation in the *Severance* universe.

A Joint Victory

In order to realize Erickson's vision, Severance's casting was crucial. Adam Scott portrays the duality of a guy struggling with loss and the unnerving realities of his detached existence in a nuanced portrayal as Mark Scout. The story's emotional and thematic complexities are enhanced by the outstanding performances of the supporting ensemble, which includes Patricia Arquette, John Turturro, Christopher Walken, and Britt Lower.

Creativity flourished because of the cooperative relationship between Erickson, Stiller, and the actors. Because of his experience in both comedy and drama, Stiller was able to deftly handle *Severance's* tonal changes, striking a balance between the series' heavier themes and humorous moments. Although Erickson's screenplay served as the basis, the team's collective energy transformed the project into a cultural phenomenon.

A Timely and Resonant Story

Severance has resonated with both viewers and reviewers since its February 2022 debut on Apple TV+. In a time when work-life balance is a major problem, its examination of workplace dynamics, corporate overreach, and identity fragmentation feels especially pertinent. In addition to offering a compelling story full of mystery and suspense, the series challenges viewers to consider the morality of contemporary labor practices.

Severance's success is evidence of its skill as a storyteller. The series has solidified its status as a critical and cultural hit with 14 Primetime Emmy nominations and wins for its musical score and main title design. Severance's provocative ideas and brilliant execution continue to enthrall viewers as it gets ready to return for a much-anticipated second season in January 2025. More than just a television show, Dan Erickson's Severance is a mirror reflecting the intricacies of contemporary life. A cinematic experience that lasts long after the screen goes black, the journey into the world of Lumon Industries is both terrifying and educational.

Chapter 1: The First Season: Getting Started at Lumon Industries

Viewers are drawn into the eerie world of Lumon Industries, a company that is both powerful and mysterious, in the first season of Severance. The severance technique, which separates a person's job and personal consciousness and creates two distinct identities, is a particularly intriguing notion introduced in the series. This idea not only forms the core of the show's plot but also delves deeply into issues of ethics, autonomy, and identity. This chapter introduces us to the varied cast of characters, delves into the two lives of Lumon personnel, and reveals the dynamics that exist beneath the dark walls of the severed floor.

The premise: Employees' Dual Lives and Severance

Fundamentally, Severance investigates the psychological and ethical ramifications of the severance process. Lumon develops a distinct workforce that only lives inside the boundaries of the business environment by isolating an individual's work awareness (Innie) from their personal consciousness (Outie). The Innies' entire lives are centered around their jobs; they never leave the workplace. On the other hand, the Outies lose eight hours of their lives every day without remembering what happened, but they are completely free from stress related to their jobs.

The Innies are put at previously unheard-of risk by this bold idea. They are completely dependent on Lumon's systems and supervisors since they lack personal agency, autonomy, and historical context. Outies, on the other hand, benefit from their jobs without having to deal with the tedium or psychological effects of it. Unsettling questions are brought up by this parallel existence: Is it moral to make a version of oneself just for work? What accountability does the Outie have for the welfare of their Innie?

These conundrums are the focus of season one, which follows Mark Scout and his group as they negotiate Lumon Industries' complex regulations. The smooth separation between Innie and Outie starts to show cracks as their story progresses, revealing information that calls into question the severance program's basic tenets.

Meet the Characters and Cast

Severance's ensemble cast is its strongest point; their nuanced performances give their complicated roles depth. Let's examine the main characters from the first season and their complex interactions within the Lumon ecosystem.

Mark Scout: The Leader in Grief

Adam Scott's character Mark Scout acts as the series' emotional fulcrum. Mark, a former history professor, decides to take severance as a way to cope with his grief after losing his wife. Overwhelmed with grief, his Outie finds comfort in forgetting about the cut floor.

However, Mark's Innie starts the series in a naive state. After his friend Petey's unexplained departure, Mark was appointed as the head of the Macro Data Refinement (MDR) team. However, he finds it difficult to reconcile his increased responsibilities with his mounting disquiet over Lumon's methods. As the season goes on, Petey reappears, trying to reintegrate and reveal the truth about Lumon, drawing Mark's Outie into a web of intrigue.

Mark's journey is a moving examination of self-discovery and resiliency. His two lives illustrate the emotional cost of severance by illustrating the conflict between escape and confrontation.

Helly Riggs: The Belligerent Newcomer

The viewer enters the severed floor through Britt Lower's character, Helly Riggs: The Belligerent Newcomer. Innie, played by Helly, is abruptly thrown into the confusing world of Lumon as a new member. Helly opposes severance right away, in contrast to Mark, who has assimilated into the company culture.

One of the season's main themes is her disobedience. Helly's frequent attempts to flee, both mentally and physically, reveal the dark depth of Lumon's hold over its staff. In stark contrast to her Innie's disobedience, her Outie is exposed as a fervent advocate of severance.

The moral conundrum of severance is highlighted by Helly's storyline. Her fight for independence serves as a rallying cry for the Innies and sparks a larger uprising against Lumon's repressive government.

Burt, Irving, and Dylan: Lumon's Workforce Layers

Dylan George (Zach Cherry) joins the MDR team with a keen sense of humor and a profound respect for Lumon's corporate benefits. Under his witty façade, Dylan has a deep-seated interest about the world outside the severed floor and a fierce loyalty to his coworkers. When he finds tidbits of his Outie existence, his quest for independence and connection takes a drastic turn.

John Turturro's character Irving Bailiff stands in for Lumon's labor force's traditional leadership. Initially acting as a counterbalance to the more disobedient members of the MDR team, he is a stickler for regulations and corporate policy. Irving's romantic relationship with Burt Goodman, the head of the Optics and Design (O&D) branch, reveals that beneath his tough exterior lies a soft heart. Within the sterile walls of Lumon, their relationship provides a unique opportunity for intimacy and vulnerability.

Burt Goodman, played by Christopher Walken, is a captivating character in the series. He infuses the normally dull realm of Lumon with a feeling of artistry and subdued revolt as the commander of O&D. One moving subplot that questions the limits set by the severance process is his relationship with Irving. Their relationship turns into a symbol of defiance, highlighting the humanism that endures even the most inhumane structures.

Seth Milchick and Harmony Cobel: Severance Enforcers

Cobel Harmony (Patricia Arquette)

Lumon's pervasive power is personified by Harmony Cobel, the mysterious manager of the severed floor. She manipulates both Innies and Outies to further the company's objectives, operating with an unnerving mix of maternal affection and brutal pragmatism. Cobel gives her character an additional level of interest by posing as Mark's modest neighbor, Mrs. Selvig, outside of work.

Cobel is almost fanatically devoted to Lumon. She has a cult-like devotion to the company's creator, Kier Eagan, and her behavior frequently conflates devotion and obsession. One of the main plot points of the season is her complicated relationship with Mark, whom she both protects and takes advantage of.

Tramell Tillman's character, Seth Milchick

Corporate control is personified by Milchick, the supervisor of the severed floor. With his constant smile and eerily upbeat manner, Milchick firmly and precisely enforces Lumon's policies. He upholds order while suppressing opposition, acting as a mediator and a disciplinarian.

The subtleties of Lumon's potency are made clear by Milchick's contacts with the MDR team. His capacity to alternate between friendly companionship and stern authority highlights the psychological deception that the severance program entails.

The isolated environment of Lumon Industries is expertly created in the first season of Severance. The severed level is a mental and physical prison, with its retro-futuristic design and winding corridors. Jeremy Hindle, the production designer, created a space that is both timeless and confusing by drawing cues from modernist architecture and mid-century corporate aesthetics.

The show's visual language supports its topics. Lumon's dearth of windows and natural light is a reflection of the Innies' lack of agency and viewpoint. The artificiality of the severance gap is further highlighted by the sharp contrast between the lively, chaotic world outside and the antiseptic workplace setting. The narrative structure of the season, which is characterized by cliffhangers and slow-burning discoveries, puts fans on edge. The audience is drawn farther into Lumon's eerie mysteries with each new episode that reveals more of its secrets.

Chapter 2: Key Themes and Ethical Questions

Severance's genius is found in the deep ideas and moral dilemmas it examines, not alone in its gripping story. The first season explores the human psyche in great detail, analyzing identity, autonomy, and the ubiquitous impact of corporate power. The sharp contrast between the "Innie" and "Outie" identities and the more general philosophical issues of free will, control, and corporate domination are the two main concepts at the center of this investigation.

The Dichotomy of Innie-Outie

The technology that separates a person's consciousness into two separate personas—the Innie (workplace self) and the Outie (personal self)—is the fundamental component of the Severance method. Despite being initially offered as a practical way to achieve work-life balance, this contradiction soon displays its existential and ethical implications.

The Innie: A Work-Defined Life

For the Innies, Lumon Industries is where life starts and ends. They lack context and recollections of their identities outside of the workplace. Their responsibilities, their coworkers, and the corporate culture that is forced upon them shape every aspect of their lives. This poses difficult queries:

- *What makes a life meaningful?*

   In a sense, the Innies are born into slavery. They are deprived of the chance to develop a cohesive sense of self and lack personal initiative. The moral ramifications of fabricating a version of oneself for work alone are brought to light by the show. Is it still worthwhile to live a life devoid of context or choice?

- *The consent issue:*

  Although the Outies consent to the severance process, the Innies, who suffer the most as a result, are not given a voice in their continued existence. The ethical dangers of a system in which one self forces irrevocable decisions on another are highlighted by this asymmetry.

The Outie: Avoiding Accountability

Severance provides the Outies with a way out of the grind of labor. They benefit from their work without the usual emotional or mental toll it would take. But this distance creates a disturbing disengagement from the suffering of the Innies. Instead of seeing their Innies as extensions of themselves, outies like Helly's public image see them as tools. Personal accountability is called into doubt by this separation. Can you genuinely think of yourself as whole if one aspect of you is suffering? The Outie-Innie relationship turns into a metaphor for social indifference—how frequently do people put convenience ahead of facing the moral ramifications of their behavior?

The Slow Dismantling of the Divide

The seemingly unbreakable barrier between the Innies and Outies starts to come down as the season goes on. The lines separating the two identities are blurred in instances such as Mark's Outie investigation into Lumon and Dylan's fleeting view of his Outie life. These fissures demonstrate how unsustainable severance is. Since the human soul inherently seeks coherence and wholeness, true identity cannot be permanently divided into compartments.

Corporate Dominance, Control, and Free Will

Severance is a harsh indictment of corporate culture and its cruel inclinations beneath its futuristic concept. The program explores how companies manipulate people, undermining their independence and turning them into insignificant parts of a larger system.

The False Presence of Free Will

Lumon Industries functions under the pretense of giving its workers options and opportunities. After all, the severance process is optional. However, the series reveals this purported freedom to be a delusion.

- *Regarding the Outies:*

   Under hardship or emotional vulnerability, the decision to endure severance is frequently made. For instance, Mark Scout decides to take severance in order to avoid the sorrow of losing his wife. This brings to light a crucial moral conundrum: can a desperate decision really be regarded as free?

- *For the Innies:*

The Innies have no free will at all. Lumon controls every aspect of their existence, including the chores they complete and the feelings they are permitted to express. Lumon's harsh tactics to quell dissent are best exemplified by the breakroom, a punitive setting where rebellious workers are psychologically conditioned.

Dominance of corporations and dehumanization

A terrifying dramatization of actual corporate overreach is Lumon Industries. Employees are completely under the company's control, both within and outside of the workplace. This domination extends beyond the cut floor; Lumon blurs the boundaries between the private and professional domains by infiltrating its employees' personal life through individuals like Harmony Cobel.

Among the main components of Lumon's domination are:

- *Monitoring and manipulation:*

  Employee compliance is maintained by the continuous observation of the severed floor. This reflects worries about workplace surveillance in the real world, where workers' activities and output are being monitored more and more by technology.

- *Cult-like devotion:*

Kier Eagan, Lumon's founder, is held in almost religious awe. The symbols and rituals associated with Eagan are intended to stifle critical thought and foster loyalty. This is similar to how some businesses use their executives' cult of personality as a means of enforcing obedience.

- *The Battle for Independence*

The characters in Severance exhibit a persistent yearning for independence in spite of Lumon's repressive authority. This conflict manifests itself in a number of ways, such as Dylan's resolve to find out more about his Outie past and Helly's rejection of her

- *Outie's authority.*

  These deeds of defiance highlight how strong the human spirit is.

The issue of control affects society as a whole, not just the individual. Lumon's severance program can be interpreted as a metaphor for the more general ways that power structures try to repress uniqueness in favor of conformity and uniformity.

Intentionally Left Blank

Chapter 3: Visual Storytelling

Severance's eerie charm is derived from both its complex plot and its painstakingly created visual storytelling. The series creates a world that is both familiar and unsettling through the use of production design, cinematography, and symbolic imagery. This chapter explores how these components become essential to the show's concepts and emotional impact, going beyond simple aesthetic decisions.

Production and Cinematography Design

Composition and Framing

Severance creates a visual language from the first frame that emphasizes its themes of dominance and loneliness.

Minimalism and Symmetry

The symmetry in many of the images taken inside Lumon Industries is harsh, bordering on oppressive. This accuracy reflects the strict framework of the lives of the fired employees, where departure is neither permitted nor feasible. The use of simple, impersonal settings heightens the feeling of sterility and alienation.

- *Wide Shots and Negative Space:*

  To highlight characters who are dwarfed by their surroundings, the camera regularly moves back. These broad shots highlight Mark's inconsequence in relation to the broader mechanisms that control his existence, whether he is sitting by himself in his modest home or moving through Lumon's interminable, antiseptic halls. The huge blank space turns into a visual representation of the emptiness that both the Outies and the Innies feel in their segregated lives.

- *Color scheme and lighting*

  To further emphasize the dualism of the cut lives, the series makes use of color and lighting.

- *The Fluorescent Glow of Lumon:*

  The harsh, artificial light that floods the sliced floor creates a sense of anxiety and perpetual observation. The fact that there is no natural light reminds us that the Innies are isolated from everything, including the outside world and any organic reality.

- *Pops of Color vs. Muted Tones:*

  The workplace's control and monotony are reflected in the muted color scheme, which is dominated by whites, grays, and greens. Nonetheless, sporadic splashes of color, such as the vivid blue of the office carpet or the scarlet of the break room chair, highlight tense or important moments and gently influence the viewer's emotional reaction.

Production Design: Lumon's World

A major factor in drawing spectators into Lumon Industries' eerie world is its architectural layout.

- *The Winding Halls of Corridor:*

  The labyrinthine design of Lumon's cut floor represents the psychological and emotional captivity of its staff. Both the protagonists and the audience become confused by these endless, identical passageways, which further emphasizes the notion that there is no way out.

- *Retro-Futuristic Aesthetic:*

  Lumon's design blends futuristic technology with aspects of office culture from the 1960s and 1970s. The power dynamics at work are implied to be as old as humanity itself, implying that this anachronistic blending is ageless.

- *Sparse Personal Spaces:*

  The characters' out-of-office lives are also devoid of individuality. For example, Mark's home is just as stark and impersonal as his workplace, emphasizing the general emptiness of his life. This design decision implies that severance does not address the underlying melancholy in his existence by obfuscating the distinction between his two personalities.

The Symbolism of Technology and the Office

In Severance, the workplace and its technology are more than just locations; they are representations of power, dehumanization, and identity conflict.

- *The Workplace as a Prison*

  A prison masquerading as a business is the sliced floor. Its purpose and intent are to stifle uniqueness and impose conformity.

- *The Environment Without Windows:*

  Lumon's workplace lacks windows, which gives it a timeless feel and further distances the Innies from nature. The Innies lose even the most fundamental symbols of freedom and humanity when they are deprived of sunlight and an outside perspective.

- *Control by Ergonomics:*

  The workstations' low dividers and antiquated computers are intended to maximize output while providing the least amount of comfort. Lumon's wish to keep an eye on everything and make sure there are no deviations from the norm is reflected in the absence of privacy.

- *The Isolation Pods:*

  Areas designed for retraining or punishment, such as the wellness center and the break room, highlight how deceptive corporate control can be. Although they present themselves as safe spaces, these places are actually instruments of psychological control.

Technology as a Two-Sided Weapon

Severance's technology, which represents humanity's battle with creativity and morality, is both amazing and dangerous.

- *The Implant for Severance:*

  The ultimate infringement on personal freedom is the implant. It deprives the Innies of their humanity while providing the Outies with a break from their work-related responsibilities. There are unsettling concerns over the boundaries of technological involvement given the implant's capacity to alter identity.

- Older Computers and Equipment:

  The outdated equipment on the floor, like the green-screen PCs and analog monitors, gives the impression that things are stagnating. It implies that Lumon is stuck in the past, holding onto antiquated ideas of efficiency and control, even in spite of its sophisticated severance method.

- The Mysterious Work:

  The Innies are unable to comprehend the reason behind their labor because tasks like fine-tuning "scary numbers" on the computer are purposefully abstract. This represents the disconnection from the results of their labor that many employees experience in today's workplaces.

The Workplace as an Introspective Mirror

The severed floor is a psychological environment as much as a location of employment. The employees' disjointed identities are reflected in its design.

- *As Neural Pathways, Corridors:*

  It is possible to interpret the maze-like corridors as a metaphor for the Innies' fragmented and confused thoughts as a result of the severance process. Their battle to make sense of their lives is mirrored in their struggle to move through these hallways.

- *A Microcosm of Power Dynamics in the Conference Room:*

  When workers congregate in the central conference room for corporate indoctrination or team-building activities, it turns into a battlefield for power. The severe, almost clinical style of the space draws attention to the disparity in authority between Lumon's employees and management.

Symbolism's Use in Important Scenes

To emphasize its themes and emotional beats, the series uses visual symbolism.

- The Elevators

The elevators act as both practical and symbolic thresholds, moving workers from the severed floor to the outside world. They stand for the separation of the Innie and Outie selves and the brittle line between control and freedom.

- *The artwork and corporate propaganda:*

  Lumon's office is filled with multi-symbolic artwork. Although Kier Eagan paintings and corporate history scenes are meant to inspire loyalty, they frequently have a menacing, oppressive appearance that betrays the darker realities that lie beneath the surface.

- *Helly's Attempted Escape:*

  Brutal, unflinching images frame Helly's continuous attempts to rebel against Lumon, including her terrifying attempt at self-harm. These scenes demonstrate the human spirit's despair in the face of persistent injustice.

Severance creates an eerie and thought-provoking universe with its production design, cinematography, and symbolic usage of technology and the office. Each frame has a function that challenges viewers to consider the control structures in their own lives while engrossing them further in the story.

Chapter 4: Mysteries and Revelations of Season One

Severance thrives on its capacity to construct gripping secrets and gradually solve them through moving disclosures. By revealing the dark foundations of Lumon Industries and removing layers of intrigue, Season One puts viewers on edge. Petey's exit and its effects on the Macro Data Refinement (MDR) team, as well as the intricate relationship between the Innie and Outie lifestyles of the fired employees, are two major themes that jump out.

Petey's Departure and the Macro Data Refinement Team

Petey's Defection: A Spark for Veracity

Much of the main drama in the season is built up by Petey's abrupt departure from Lumon. His choice to go through reintegration, a risky and unproven reversal of the severance procedure, as a former member of the Macro Data Refinement team, represents the first rift in Lumon's tightly controlled façade.

- *Reintegration and the Effects It Has:*

  Petey's post-reintegration state is both shocking and enlightening. The psychological toll of trying to combine two lives that were forcibly divided is highlighted by his jumbled recollections and unpredictable actions. This acts as a terrifying reminder of the harm that the separation process causes.

- *The Map and Hidden Truths:*

  Petey creates a physical representation of his revolt by mapping the floor that has been cut off. A pivotal moment in the season, this act of disobedience implies that resistance is possible even inside Lumon's repressive system. The map also emphasizes how the floor was cut off, both literally and figuratively, symbolizing the employees' attempt to reconcile their disparate identities.

The Macro Data Refinement Team: Relationships in the Face of Mysteries

The ambiguity surrounding the MDR team's work reflects Lumon Industries' larger secrets.

- *The type of work:*

  The goal of their labor is called into doubt by the purposefully abstract nature of the task of refining "scary numbers." Do their seemingly random tasks have a darker purpose, or are they just cogs in a bigger, unknown machine? The ambiguity surrounding their work is a metaphor for the dehumanization and alienation that characterize contemporary business settings.

- *Team Dynamics:*

The MDR team builds sincere relationships in spite of the repressive nature of their surroundings. A dynamic interplay of tension and companionship is created by the unique personalities and motivations that Mark, Helly, Dylan, and Irving each offer. Within Lumon's dehumanizing confines, their common experiences and tiny acts of defiance—like Dylan's joy in finding "perks" like finger traps—offer glimmers of humanity.

- *Petey's Absence:*

Petey's exit creates a hole in the squad, highlighting how crucial their relationships are. Their workflow is affected by his absence, and they are also becoming more conscious of the wider ramifications of their broken lives.

The Overlap of Innie and Outie Lives

Severance's examination of the shaky line between the fired employees' Innie and Outie identities is among its most captivating features. The overlap between these seemingly distinct lives becomes more noticeable as the season goes on, highlighting Lumon's system's fundamental weaknesses.

The Severed Employees' Dual Identities

Lumon's workers' personal and professional lives are sharply separated by the separation process. This distinction is not smooth nor definitive, though.

- *The Two Griefs of Mark Scout:*

  Mark's battle to deal with the loss of his wife, Gemma, defines his Outie life. Even though his Innie isn't aware of this loss, his attitude at work reflects the general melancholy of his Outie life. This emotional bleed-through implies that the intricacies of human feeling cannot be completely eliminated by the severance technique.

- Helly's Rebellion:

As an Innie, Helly's rebellion is a result of her refusal to comply with Lumon's restrictions. The conflict between self-preservation and self-liberation is highlighted by Her Outie's insistence on upholding the severance procedure, which adds another level of complexity. The moral consequences of severance are shown in the startling scene where Helly's Outie makes her view a film that denies her requests for release.

The Function of the Subconscious and Memory

Instances where memories and emotions seem to cross the gap cast doubt on the severance barrier's purported impermeability.

- *Symptoms of Petey's Reintegration:*

  According to Petey's post-reintegration hallucinations, severance only suppresses memories rather than erasing them. Lumon's technology's psychological toll is demonstrated by the chaotic overlap between his Innie and Outie personalities caused by the reappearance of these memories.

- *Irving's Dreams and Paintings:*

  Irving's fixation with gloomy, menacing paintings of hallways, which reflect Innie's experiences on the severed floor, is a defining feature of his Outie life. The human mind resists artificial compartmentalization, as suggested by this subconscious connection, which also suggests that the severance barrier is porous.

Lumon's Identity Manipulation

Lumon's hold on its workers permeates not just their broken lives but also their Outie lives.

- *Harmony Cobel's Monitoring:*

  The degree of Lumon's infiltration is demonstrated by Cobel's surreptitious involvement in Mark's Outie life while posing as his neighbor Mrs. Selvig. Her dual position highlights the company's readiness to conflate identities and blur lines for its own benefit.

- *The Audiovisual Messages:*

  Lumon reinforces the distinction between Innies and Outies by using pre-recorded messages. As demonstrated by Helly's interactions with her Outie, these videos frequently have a spooky undertone. Employees are further dehumanized by the scripted structure of these conversations, which reduces their identities to corporate constructions.

The Moments of Breakthrough

The moments where the lives of Innie and Outie converge, leading to disclosures that call into question Lumon's authority, define the conclusion of Season One.

- *Dylan's Giving Up:*

  A pivotal moment in the story occurs when Dylan decides to switch on the overtime contingency, enabling the Innies to momentarily occupy their

Outie bodies. The Innies' developing consciousness and agency are demonstrated by their act of rebellion, which also highlights Lumon's system's fundamental shortcomings.

- The final revelation that Mark's wife, Gemma, is still alive and employed at Lumon under the alias Ms. Casey profoundly blurs the boundaries between Mark's Innie and Outie existence. In addition to adding to the mystery, this turn of events calls into doubt Lumon's actual intentions and the morality of its deeds.

Chapter 5: Season Two - Expanding the Narrative

Severance's sophomore season bears the burden of higher expectations after its captivating premiere. With new mysteries, developing character arcs, and a more thorough examination of Lumon Industries' sinister schemes, Season Two broadens the scope of the story. Behind the scenes, there were significant obstacles and changes in the planning and production process, and the series' course was shaped by fresh creative voices.

Development and Production of Season Two

Overcoming Obstacles from Postponements to Resumptions

The process of producing Season Two was far from easy. Its development was impacted by both internal and external influences, such as logistical challenges, worldwide interruptions, and innovative recalibrations.

- *Worldwide Difficulties and Postponements:*

  The production schedule was first delayed by the worldwide COVID-19 pandemic, which had a lasting impact on the entertainment sector. Creative changes were required due to strict health and safety regulations, especially when it came to handling larger-scale sequences and creating intimate scenes.

- *Labor Strikes and Their Effects:*

  One noteworthy development was the dramatic change in Hollywood's labor scene, which included strikes by writers and actors that had an immediate effect on Severance. In addition to delaying production, these industry-wide events highlighted the actors and crew's contributions to the series. The strikes emphasized the value of equitable pay and artistic freedom, which was consistent with the labor and control themes of the series.

- *Overcoming Setbacks:*

  The Severance team showed resilience in the face of these difficulties. With newfound energy, filming got underway again, using creative methods to preserve the show's unique look. The production team's flexibility was demonstrated by the use of remote collaboration technologies, smaller crew configurations, and spaced shooting schedules.

- *Changing the Vision:*

  The creators unintentionally used the delays to improve the storyline of the season. The authors were able to develop character arcs, complicate the main storyline, and introduce new conceptual layers into the narrative with more time for brainstorming and editing.

The Impact of Up-and-Coming Authors and Directors

The introduction of new creative talent was one of the biggest changes in Season Two. While preserving the series' essential identity, new writers and directors enhanced it with their varied viewpoints and creative storytelling approaches.

New Authors: Broadening the Narrative's Purview

- *Extending the Subjects:*

  Season Two delves into subjects beyond the boundaries of Lumon Industries, as new authors join the crew. More attention is paid to issues like structural inequality, the psychological effects of corporate allegiance, and the philosophical ramifications of memory manipulation. The show's relevancy is further increased by these additions, which speak to current situations.

- *Character-Driven Storytelling:*

  The new authors placed a high priority on character growth, exploring the underlying struggles, motives, and backstories of important characters. Helly's rebellious spirit encounters complex obstacles, Mark's grief process assumes additional dimensions, and Irving's relationship with Burt is examined in greater depth. Viewers are able to develop stronger emotional bonds with the ensemble group because of this character-centric approach.

- *Dynamic Dialogue and Humor:*

  Severance is known for its witty, frequently sinister humor. While adding more nuanced layers of wit and sarcasm, the new writing team maintained this tone. This well-rounded strategy guarantees that the program will maintain its distinct voice even as the stakes increase.

New Directors: A New Language of Visuals

- *Extending the Color Scheme:*

  Although Season One developed a unique visual style characterized by antiseptic, austere settings and unnerving symmetry, Season Two expands on this palette. In order to capture the evolving dynamics of the story, new filmmakers play around with color grading, lighting, and camera angles. The starker contrast between the cut floor and the outside world represents the growing distance between the protagonists' two lives.

- *Innovative Storytelling Techniques:*

  The new directors also use non-traditional storytelling techniques, such as abstract montages, dream sequences, and non-linear timelines. These strategies heighten the show's psychological curiosity and enhance its strange feel. Scenes where Innie and Outie's realities are blurred, for instance, use distorted images and fragmented editing to create a sense of confusion.

- *Emphasis on World-Building:*

  Season Two introduces new locales and delves deeper into Lumon's wider impact than just the sliced floor. From intimidating corporate headquarters to creepy research labs, the directors carefully craft these environments to reflect the company's pervasiveness. The atmospheric tension of the series is enhanced by each locale, which functions as a character unto itself.

Working Together with New and Old Voices

The collaborative culture that the show's original creators promoted made it easy to incorporate new talent. To maintain consistency, the newcomers collaborated closely with the show's creator, Dan Erickson, and producer and director Ben Stiller, who continues to be a major presence.

- *Keeping Things Continuous:*

    The creative styles of new and returning team members were bridged through collaborative writing sessions and thorough storyboards. The series' unique tone and narrative coherence were preserved thanks to this strategy.

- *Promoting Innovation:*

  Some of the season's most memorable moments came from the veterans' encouragement of the new squad members to take innovative chances. An important episode that includes a business banquet, for example, demonstrates the directors' talent at choreographing elaborate, high-stakes scenes.

Season Two: An Extension of the Story

Season Two not only met but surpassed expectations thanks to a mix of thoughtfully delayed production, new creative voices, and a shared dedication to excellence.

- New Mysteries and Alliances:

  Season Two presents a number of fascinating subplots, including the establishment of an underground resistance movement and the discovery of a secret department within Lumon. These changes broaden the scope of the story while preserving Severance's personal, character-driven focus.

- *More Complex Ethical Issues:*

  The season explores the philosophical ramifications of severance and how it affects ideas of morality, autonomy, and identity. These discussions are made more complex by the addition of new characters, such as a whistleblower from Lumon's higher levels.

- *Elevated Stakes:*

  As the protagonists learn more about Lumon's long-term intentions, their challenges become more pressing. In particular, the season finale significantly ups the ante, laying the groundwork for a thrilling third season.

Chapter 6: In-Depth Analysis of Episodes from Season Two

Building on the success of its first season, Severance's second season offers viewers an exciting blend of character growth, narrative progression, and provocative ideas. The characters' complex lives and more of Lumon Industries' sinister secrets are revealed in each episode, which functions as a puzzle piece. This chapter examines how the plots develop, how the characters grow, and how fresh ideas and turns lead the program to new heights.

Evolving Character Arcs and Storylines

A Leader Split Between Two Worlds: Mark Scout

The show's emotional center is Mark's journey in Season Two. He is even more driven to pursue the truth after learning about Lumon's manipulation of his Innie and Outie personas.

- *Reclaiming Agency:*

  As Mark's Outie starts to piece together the hints Petey left behind, he finds documents and mysterious messages that allude to the scope of Lumon's power. In the meantime, Innie assumes a leadership position inside the Macro Data Refinement (MDR) team, motivating them to oppose.

- Key Episode:

  The company's enforcers are forced to face the Macrodata team after Mark's Innie inserts erroneous data into Lumon's systems, resulting in a tense confrontation. This episode demonstrates Mark's increasing self-assurance as a leader.

- *Personal Revelations:*

  Mark's reasons for having the surgery and the depth of his sadness over his wife's passing are made clear by flashbacks to his life prior to severance. But clues that Lumon might have contributed to her death strengthen his determination to destroy them.

Helly Riggs: The Unwilling Pioneer

Helly's storyline changes from that of a disobedient newcomer to that of a key player in the resistance. Her internal struggle between her resistance as an Innie and her submission as an Outie intensifies.

- *Balancing Act:*

  It turns out that Helly's Outie is a driven businessman connected to Lumon's board. Innie is shocked by this revelation and struggles with the possibility that her Outie is involved in Lumon's plots.

- *Key Episode:*

  Helly's Innie briefly accesses her Outie's memories in a terrifying incident, allowing her to witness firsthand the life she is powerless to control.

Burt, Dylan, and Irving: Novel Aspects of Known Faces

- *Irving's Search for Connection:*

  A major plotline revolves around Irving's attempt to get back in touch with Burt. His own mysterious history with the corporation is revealed when he learns the truth about Lumon's dominance over staff relationships.

- *Key Episode:*

  In a moving episode, Irving and Burt collaborate to look into Lumon's classified divisions; their growing friendship serves as a ray of hope during the darker parts of the season.

- *Dylan's Sacrifice:*

  In Season One, Dylan struggles with the fallout from his choices, especially his part in revealing the severance program. His desire to keep his family safe as a father pushes him to take more daring chances.

Exploring New Themes and Twists

While adhering to its philosophical foundation, Season Two broadens the show's scope by including a variety of subjects and plot twists.

Novel Themes

- *Technology Ethics and Corporate Overreach:*

  Season Two explores the societal effects of severance, while Season One examined the personal ramifications. It is discovered that Lumon's severance technology is a component of a broader business plan meant to impact healthcare, education, and politics.

- *Key Point:*

  Mark and Helly's Outies unintentionally testify on opposing sides of a severance technology government inquiry that included public arguments.

- *Identity and Memory as Commodities:*

  Lumon's experiments with memory manipulation go beyond severance, suggesting that they may be able to create, restore, or implant memories. This calls into question whether personal experiences are truly authentic.

- *Key Point:*

  In a terrifying revelation, Lumon is seen experimenting with "hybrid" workers whose memories are completely made up.

- *The Price of Resistance:*

  The characters pay a personal price for their increasing opposition to Lumon. Season Two explores if the goals outweigh the methods and how far people would go to regain their independence.

Major Twists

- *The Eagan Legacy:*

  As their impact on Lumon and society at large is examined, the history of the Eagan family takes center stage. The stakes are raised considerably with the arrival of a new enemy, a charming but vicious heir to the Eagan family.

- *The Real Goal of the Severance Procedure:*

  The severance procedure was initially created for military applications, as revealed in a startling mid-season twist. Lumon's ultimate objective is to turn memory manipulation into a weapon, raising moral questions regarding its application in combat.

- *Crossing the Line:*

  Innie and Outie's barrier is broken for the first time. In a pivotal scene, Mark's Innie completely becomes part of his Outie's life, feeling both liberated and utterly lost. Lumon is enraged by this incident, but it also gives other Innies hope.

The Climax Arc of the Season

Season Two's penultimate episodes are filled with high-stakes confrontations, betrayals, and revelations. Now a full-fledged resistance group, the Macro Data Refinement team breaks into Lumon's top-secret lab to reveal its activities. A conflict with Lumon officials results from Mark's Outie's inability to reconcile his memories with Innie's information.

The season finale keeps spectators on the edge of their seats, with multiple cliffhangers:

- Helly's Innie takes possession of her Outie's body during a live corporate gala, revealing Lumon's severance program to the world.
- Irving discovers a link between Lumon and his own family's history, suggesting he was groomed for severance from an early age.
- Mark is faced with a terrible decision: risk losing his newfound independence or forming a risky partnership to destroy Lumon.

Chapter 7 : Lumon Industries: The Growing Mythos

More than just a business, Lumon Industries is a maze of secrets and a representation of unbridled ambition shrouded in ceremonial awe. In Season Two, the mysterious business, which serves as the foundation of Severance, develops its mythos and unveils new levels of mystery that strengthen its hold on the story. This chapter examines how Kier Eagan and the mysterious Severed Floor create a cult of personality and how Lumon is transformed from an antagonist to a living, breathing mystery.

Kier Eagan's Cult of Personality

Is the Eagan Legacy Tyrant or Visionary?

The founder Kier Eagan, whose ideas form the foundation of Lumon's culture and business practices, is at the center of the company's mystique. Even though Kier passed away a long time ago, his presence still looms big as a messianic figure among his followers and staff. His image hangs on workplace walls, his words are paraphrased like holy texts, and Lumon's destiny is shaped by his legacy.

- *Kier's Theory:*

  Season Two of the show delves deeper into Kier's writings, which combine business jargon with overtly religious overtones. Workers learn to respect him as a visionary who used new technology to *"perfect humanity,"* eliminating imperfections and increasing output. However, as the spectator gets a glimpse of Kier's fixation with obedience and control, his utopian goals start to feel more ominous.

- *The Cultish Devotion:*

  Kier's mythology is reinforced through rituals performed on Lumon staff members. These include corporate festivals honoring his accomplishments, morning recitations, and the spooky *"Kier Appreciation Hours,"* during which staff members get very intimate praise for their contributions.

- *Key Scene:*

  Kier leads an early prototype of the Severance program in a dreamlike flashback, persuading test subjects of its ethical and spiritual necessity. His charm is evident, but so is his cruelty, as he sacrifices people to achieve perfection.

The Eagan Family's Grip on Lumon

Season Two examines how Kier's ancestors continue to dominate him by playing with his mythology. In order to further their own goals and protect the public from Kier's more sinister realities, the Eagan family acts as both stewards and exploiters of his legacy.

- *A Split Heir:*

  Complexity is increased by the arrival of a new member of the Eagan family—a disobedient, reform-minded heir. This individual initially presents themselves as a resistance supporter but eventually displays contradictory allegiances, divided between upholding and destroying their family's dominion.

Kier as a Control Symbol

Kier's cult of personality accomplishes two goals: it diverts Lumon's employees from doubting their independence and unites them under a common set of beliefs. Lumon ensures that workers view opposition as blasphemy by elevating compliance to a moral obligation through the deification of its founder.

- *Viewer Implications:*

  Kier's storyline calls into question charismatic leadership and contemporary organizations. To what extent is our faith in leaders based on true beliefs, and to what extent is it fabricated by well constructed myths?

The Severed Floor's Secrets

The Mysteries of the Severed Floor

Only terminated personnel can visit the Severed Floor, a remote area of Lumon Industries that was first shown in Season One. Although its presence is unnerving, Season Two makes it a major mystery by exposing its darker intent and terrifying ramifications.

- *An Isolated Experiment:*

  The Severed Floor serves as a testing ground in addition to a workspace. Extreme psychological circumstances are used to terminate employees in experimental departments located on the floor. Lumon uses the Severed Floor to hone its grasp on the human psyche through anything from memory implantation experiments to artificially created loyalty.

- *Key Revelation*:

  As a result of Irving's research, the crew learns that *"Beta Units,"* or workers who never leave their severed state, reside on the Severed Floor. These people are completely engrossed in Lumon's made-up universe and are not aware of the outside world.

The Relationship of the Macrodata and the Refinement Team

The MDR group discovers how they are related to the Severed Floor. Records show that their refined data is utilized to control workers at this level, continuing the tests without their awareness.

- *Helly's Finding:*

  Helly discovers a file with a list of fired workers who "*failed*" the program, their memories wiped out forever. Her name appears on the list, suggesting that her involvement with the MDR team is a component of a larger Lumon plot.

Visual Design and Symbolism

The aesthetics of Lumon's other areas stand in sharp contrast to the Severed Floor. The Severed Floor appears disorganized and eerie, in contrast to the clean and organized office above. A sense of fear is evoked by dim lighting, haphazard layouts, and mysterious symbols painted on walls.

Symbolic Elements

- *The Infinite Hall:*

  The maze-like corridor that links departments is a recurrent theme. Its seemingly limitless vastness reflects the imprisonment of the workforce.

- *The Totems*

  In a world that is intended to deprive them of their uniqueness, workers on the Severed Floor use odd items as markers of their identity.

An Epiphany Moment

The scene where Mark and Irving sneak into the Severed Floor is a climax. The breadth of Lumon's contempt for human life is revealed when they discover a vast archive that has documents of every employee who has been fired as well as their "performance ratings." Among these documents are terrifying footage of tests done on early fired employees.

- *Emotional Impact:* Mark links his personal loss to Lumon's heinous actions after discovering a file that suggests his wife may have been the subject of experimentation on the Severed Floor.

The Severed Floor, Kier, and the Overarching Image

The Severed Floor and Kier's cult of personality together serve as the two main pillars of Lumon's power: technological domination and ideological control. The Severed Floor offers the means to impose allegiance, while Kier's deification guarantees it.

Philosophical Implications

The program challenges viewers with the following elements:

How much liberty are we prepared to give up for convenience or advancement?

Is it ever possible for systemic loyalty and personal autonomy to coexist?

What occurs when gaining control becomes the ultimate objective?

Predicting Future Battles

An impending conflict was set in motion by the increasing disclosures of Kier's actual nature and the Severed Floor. The uprising of the Macro Data Refinement team is now about destroying a whole system that was created to imprison minds, not just about their personal liberation.

- *Season Finale Tease:* A mysterious note left by a renegade worker from the Severed Floor at the end of the season raises the possibility that severance technology has far-reaching effects outside of Lumon.

Chapter 8: Behind the Scenes

A show as complex and thought-provoking as Severance is the result of a single vision combined with a variety of artistic and personal inspirations. Severance's developer, Dan Erickson, created the eerily engrossing world of Lumon Industries by drawing on his own experiences, philosophical insights, and painstaking storytelling. The beginnings of Severance are examined in this chapter, along with Erickson's creative process and the life events that influenced the narrative.

The Vision of Dan Erickson

The Origins of Severance

Severance was a nagging dilemma about work-life balance in a world growing more and more detached before it became a cultural phenomena.

The Genesis of the Concept:

According to Erickson, Severance was first implemented as a reaction to the contemporary workplace. While Erickson was employed in corporate settings, where he observed the routine and emotional distance of office culture, the concept began to take shape. Severance, or the complete separation of work and personal life, originated as a parody of workplace regulations that encouraged workers to *"leave their work at the office."*

- *Key Takeaway:*

    Erickson considered how ridiculous this idea was. What would be left of our identities if we could actually separate work from life? Would we become more free or lose a piece of who we are?

Lumon Industries' Origins:

The imaginary megacorporation Lumon came to represent all of Erickson's concerns and criticisms of contemporary workplaces, including dehumanization, blind allegiance, and the value placed on productivity above individuality. The organization's customs, ceremonies, and structures were inflated representations of actual events that Erickson witnessed or encountered.

A Decade in the Making

Severance was first developed as a short tale by Erickson years before it was adapted for the big screen. It developed into a complete story over time. But perseverance was needed to make the idea a reality. Erickson waited for the ideal moment for years while honing the script and pitching it.

- *The Breakthrough Moment:*

  Ben Stiller was captivated by Erickson's writing in 2016 because of its dark humor and creative ideas. Stiller's passion for the project served as the impetus for Severance's development from a concept to a complete television series.

Personal Experiences That Influenced the Story

The Business Experience of Erickson

Before entering the entertainment business, Erickson worked a variety of day jobs, as is common for creatives. He was exposed to the tedium, monotony, and occasionally bizarre culture of the contemporary office throughout his time working in corporate positions.

- *Using the Ordinary as a Source of Motivation:*

  According to Erickson, the show's elements were inspired by routine chores like data entry and repeated procedures. Sorting unintelligible numbers was one of the Macro Data Refinement team's enigmatic responsibilities, which mirrored the sense of alienation he experienced while carrying out activities without comprehending their larger goal.

- *Office Dynamics:*

  The interactions within Lumon mirror Erickson's insights concerning office hierarchy and camaraderie. The Macro Data Refinement team's friendship exemplifies the peculiar closeness that may develop between coworkers, even in a confining setting.

Identity and Memory Themes

Personal introspection is another source of Erickson's interest in memory and identity. His personal anxieties and concerns about selfhood were tapped into by the notion of separating one's consciousness—making separate "*selves*" for work and home.

- *Compartmentalization's Human Cost:*

  According to Erickson, people frequently compartmentalize their feelings and repress aspects of themselves in order to conform to social or professional norms. This propensity is dramatized by severance, which forces characters and spectators to face the repercussions of losing one's complete identity.

- *Philosophical Influences:*

  Erickson's writing is influenced by existential philosophy, namely the writings of philosophers such as Jean-Paul Sartre and Søren Kierkegaard. His philosophical thoughts are reflected in the story's interwoven themes of alienation, free will, and the pursuit of meaning.

Individual Relationships with Grief and Loss

One of the show's key themes is Mark Scout's character growth, especially his sorrow over his wife's passing. Erickson has talked about using his personal loss experiences to influence Mark's path.

- *Using Stories to Express Emotions:*

  In Severance, Erickson examines mourning, which is a reflection of the larger issue of escape. Mark made the decision to take severance in order to avoid the suffering in his personal life as well as to maintain a work-life balance. The show's speculative components are grounded in profoundly human concerns thanks to this emotional detail.

Working Together: Developing the Severance Universe

Cooperating with the Team and Ben Stiller

Though it started as Erickson's idea, Severance developed by teamwork. As the project's director and executive producer, Ben Stiller contributed his own sensibility, which helped to counterbalance the film's somber subjects with human and humorous moments.

- *Visual Storytelling:*

  Erickson's script was enhanced by Stiller's direction, which used visuals to illustrate the concepts of the narrative. In keeping with Erickson's initial vision, the show's tone is influenced by the sterile office setting, unnerving symmetry, and bizarre production design.

The Impact of the Cast and Crew

Erickson has given the actors and crew credit for giving his characters and concepts more nuance. The performers' performances enhanced the story's emotional relevance by adding levels of complexity, especially Adam Scott's portrayal of Mark Scout.

- *Improvised Moments:*

    Collaborative experimentation on set produced some of the most memorable scenes in the show. Severance stayed lively and captivating because of Erickson's readiness to modify and develop his narrative.

The Personal Risks of Severance

Severance is more than simply a TV program to Erickson; it's a very personal endeavor that captures his existential concerns and artistic aspirations. The series is a reflection on what it means to be human as well as a critique of contemporary workplace culture.

- *A Note to the Viewers:*

  According to Erickson, he hopes *Severance* inspires viewers to consider their own life. Do we live lives that are fragmented by corporate or societal expectations, or are we completely present in our identities?

- *Legacy and Development:*

  Erickson's position in the canon of contemporary storytelling is cemented by his creation of Severance, which continues to strike a chord with audiences. In addition to establishing him as a visionary author, the series provides a platform for additional investigation into the intricate subjects he is so fervently interested in.

Chapter 9: The Creative Contributions of Ben Stiller

Ben Stiller, who is well-known for directing and playing humorous parts in movies like *Tropic Thunder* and *Zoolander*, took on a completely different task when he agreed to helm Severance. Stiller, who is renowned for his wit and incisiveness, was instrumental in transforming Severance's intricate, darkly humorous, and very emotional plot into an aesthetically spectacular and emotionally stirring television series. This chapter examines Stiller's artistic contributions to Severance, including his production and directing insights and his role in creating an emotionally charged and eerie environment.

Insights on Direction and Production

A Different Path for Ben Stiller

Severance was a big change from Ben Stiller's prior work when he was first asked to direct it. The series required a director who could strike a balance between humor and gravity, surrealism and reality, because it combined business satire, psychological suspense, and dystopian sci-fi. Stiller was the ideal person to handle this challenging tonal terrain because of his background directing incisive, character-driven comedy.

- *Addressing the Show's Dark Themes:*

    Stiller recognized the significance of tone right away. The story of Severance, which explored memory and identity, the separation of one's personal and professional lives, and the dismal farce of contemporary corporate life, required a careful balancing act between humor, tension, and melancholy. Because of his experience in comedy, Stiller was able to add lighthearted, frequently darkly ridiculous, moments that both relieve and heighten the show's sarcastic edge. However, he never downplayed the story's emotional and unnerving elements, making sure the audience understood the significance of the psychological issues at work.

- *Working together with Dan Erickson:*

Stiller's collaboration with Severance's inventor, Dan Erickson, was essential in determining the course of the program. While acknowledging Erickson's vision for the series, Stiller also contributed his own ideas, particularly about tempo and visual storytelling. With Erickson's screenplays providing the framework of the plot and Stiller directing the performances and tone, the two worked together to help create the show's aesthetic. In addition to embracing Erickson's darker moments, Stiller made room for vulnerability, which is essential to giving the characters on the show a genuine sense.

- *Making Severance a Visual Experience:*

Stiller knew that Lumon Industries' eerie corporate backdrop needed to feel like a separate character in the narrative, so he approached the series with an eye for eye-catching visuals. The chilly, symmetrical architecture, the sterile, geometric office space design, and the unsettling color schemes all added to the feeling of confusion and loneliness. Under Stiller's direction, the sets served as more than just scenery; they were an essential part of the story, enhancing the characters' experiences of alienation and imprisonment.

Production Choices and Difficulties

Severance's production was not without its challenges, especially in achieving the show's strict pacing and austere visual aesthetic. It was difficult for Stiller and the crew to strike a balance between a lofty notion and the practicalities of filmmaking. Stiller's steady hand made sure the show's vision held up in spite of these challenges.

- *Location Vs Studio Filming:*

  Although a large portion of Severance's distinctive appearance—the strictly controlled office setting—was accomplished through set design, the majority of the filming took place on location in New York. A smooth transition between the remote, dystopian environment of Lumon Industries and the real world was the goal of Stiller and the production design team. Stiller always made sure that the set complemented the narrative's thematic themes, and the series' use of cramped areas, sharp lines, and repetition in set design paralleled the characters' own psychological states.

- *Creating a Complex Atmosphere on a Limited Budget:*

Despite having a sizable budget, Severance never overspent on its elaborate production values or special effects. Stiller's direction placed a strong emphasis on nuance and restraint, making sure that atmosphere, not ostentatious action scenes, was used to build the story's tension. Without resorting to overpowering visual spectacle, Stiller created a claustrophobic universe by emphasizing minute elements, such as the office's flickering lights or the impersonal, sterile hallways.

Creating a Visual and Emotional Atmosphere

The Value of Using Pictures to Tell Stories

Severance's use of visual storytelling to complement and frequently reflect the characters' psychological states is among its most remarkable features. Stiller's painstaking attention to the series' aesthetic lets viewers solve a visual and emotional puzzle out of a simple office drama.

- *Utilizing Lighting and Color:*

    The emotional tone of Severance was largely established by color. The sterile grays and whites of Lumon Industries' offices serve as a visual representation of the dehumanization of the workers. These subdued hues stand in stark contrast to the livelier, more intense scenes that take place outside of the office, such those that show Mark's private life. Darker, murky lighting is employed to accentuate the sense of mystery and danger surrounding the Severance process, while clinical, chilly office lighting evokes a sense of emotional numbness. Stiller was able to deliver the story without depending entirely on words because of these visual cues.

- *The Geometry of the Office:*

Using symmetric spaces and geometric patterns around the office was another aspect that Stiller made come to life. The inflexibility of the characters' life at Lumon Industries was reflected in the set design's stiff, almost dystopian quality. In addition to supporting the notion of a sterile, regulated setting, the recurring visual elements also spoke to the protagonists' internal conflict. This visual language was crucial to conveying the oppressive character of the corporate environment they lived in and was used to support the idea of people who were physically, emotionally, and cognitively caught in a loop.

Creating Visual Moments Focused on Characters

Stiller's direction was especially successful at producing visually arresting scenes that let us comprehend the characters on a deeper level. One of the show's most impactful scenes, for instance, is when Mark's Innie self starts to doubt his life; this scene is accompanied with confusing and bizarre camera angles. Mark's psychological turmoil as he tries to make sense of his dual personal and professional identities is reflected in the visual instability. These character-driven scenes, in which the visual experience corresponds with the characters' emotional or psychological experiences, turned into some of the series' most memorable moments.

- *The Application of Reflection and Mirrors:*

  In order to further highlight the characters' dual nature, Stiller also employed mirrors and reflections. Moments where Mark confronts his reflection, in particular, graphically depict his battle with his dual identities—his Innie and Outie sides. These instances highlight Mark's broken sense of self by obfuscating the distinction between work and home life. Similarly, mirrors are employed to highlight the protagonists' feelings of loneliness and separation in both their personal and professional life.

- *A Subtle Approach to Surrealism:*

  Even though Severance has surrealistic aspects, Stiller handled this part of the program subtly. He anchored the program in the viewpoints of its characters rather than depending on explicitly magical images, letting the bizarre, dreamlike aspects arise from their mental states. Without alienating the audience, this controlled technique increased the audience's sensation of dread and discomfort.

The Score and Soundtrack

In order to produce a soundtrack that would go well with the show's themes and visual aesthetic, Stiller also worked with composer Theodore Shapiro. Severance's soundtrack is essential to creating suspense and emotional depth, emphasizing significant scenes with a sense of dread or melancholy. Shapiro and Stiller collaborated extensively to make sure the score complemented the mood he intended to establish, a sonic landscape that increased the series' emotional and psychological impact.

Intentionally Left Blank

Chapter 10: Creating the World of Severance

Severance's painstakingly constructed universe, which is both realistically based and uncannily fantastical, is one of its distinguishing features. The physical and artistic aspects of the show's design are crucial to drawing viewers into its apocalyptic plot. The world of Severance is aesthetically rich and profoundly symbolic, from the clinical, harsh architecture of Lumon Industries to the deliberate choices made for the costumes and sets. This chapter explores the series' main design components, including the use of architecture, props, and costumes to improve the show's examination of memory, identity, and the psychological effects of corporate domination while also creating a unique atmosphere.

Costumes, Props, and Architecture

The icy, dystopian workplace

One notable aspect of Severance is Lumon Industries' architecture, which serves as a metaphor for the dehumanizing forces operating within the company as well as a physical environment. The show's austere, symmetrical, and sterile architecture is purposefully unsettling. The company's cold, calculating attitude toward its workers is reflected in these design decisions, which eliminate uniqueness in favor of control and efficiency.

- *The Character of The Office:*

  One of the best ways to portray the notions of alienation and detachment is through Lumon Industries' architecture. The office areas are claustrophobic and eerily detached. With the exception of the delicate geometric designs that adorn them, the walls are frequently blank, which highlights how repetitious the employees' work lives are. A sensation of anxiety fills the entire room as the ceiling lights flicker menacingly. The impression of a corporate setting where workers are caught in a never-ending loop of monotony is reinforced by long corridors and bleak passageways.

- *Workplace Layout Symbolism:*

The sterile, homogeneous workplace environments further emphasize the psychological gap between the *"Innie"* and *"Outie"* lives of the staff. The staff members are restricted to their assigned departments, which are segregated from one another. The environment itself turns into a metaphor for the employees' shattered identities. The characters' emotional seclusion and the rigid divisions between their personal and professional lives are symbolized by the open but divided areas. Every area of the office is intended to arouse feelings of surveillance and compliance, reflecting the ways Lumon manipulates the ideas and behaviors of its employees.

The Props: Instruments of Identity and Control

Severance's props are more than just practical; they contribute to the show's broader thematic investigation of identity, memory, and control. The characters' tools and possessions frequently function as extensions of their positions within the organization, and occasionally they serve as both subjugating and empowering instruments.

- *The button for overtime contingency:*

  The Overtime Contingency button is among Severance's most important and visually arresting props. When workers are "*finished*" with their labor for the day, they press this big red button, which is a potent symbol of both freedom and captivity. On the one hand, it gives workers a feeling of autonomy over their professional lives. However, it also acts as a reminder of Lumon's corporate structure's repressive nature, which purposefully blurs the boundaries between work and home life. The characters' lack of agency and being torn between two identities that are in conflict with one another are symbolized by the button.

- *The Innie-Outie Device:*

  Another important prop is the Innie-Outie Device, which physically divides the Innies from their Outies. The "*severance*" process is both symbolic and physical; the device enacts the split of the employees' identities and memories. Its clinical, streamlined style embodies Lumon Industries' impersonal, invasive, and efficient corporate philosophy. The existence of the device in each employee's life acts as a reminder of their diminished independence and the psychological costs associated with leading a fragmented and half-remembered life.

- *Personal belongings:*

The employees' limited personal belongings are thoughtfully chosen to act as subtly noticeable reminders of their changed or lost identities. For instance, the only things that serve as anchors to Mark's "Outie" self are his wedding ring and a photo of his late wife, which symbolize his personal life. Throughout the series, these items acquire emotional significance, particularly when Mark's relationship with his "Outie" character grows more strained.

Costumes: A Controlling Uniform

Another important component that contributes to the setting and character definition in Severance is the costumes. The purposeful blandness and corporateness of Lumon Industries' employees' wardrobe selections support the idea of identity suppression. The distinction between the characters' actual identities and the personalities they are compelled to adopt at work is highlighted by the show's clothes.

The Use of Uniforms as a Sign of Conformity

The outfits worn by Lumon personnel are the same: khaki slacks, button-up shirts, and shoes that appear to be interchangeable. The lack of individualism within the corporate organization is symbolized by the uniforms. These boring attire visually support the perception that the employees are simply *"cogs in a machine."* Lumon's objective of assembling a workforce devoid of individuality and past experiences is reflected in the homogeneity. These clothes remove the employees' basic sense of self, leaving them anonymous workers who carry out tasks without question. It's not just their memories that are lost.

- *Character-Specific Variations:*

  Although the overall uniform is the same, minor differences in how the characters dress provide nuanced information about who they are. For example, Mark's uniform is frequently a little rumpled, which serves as a visible depiction of his inner turmoil and the emotional toll his work takes on him. Helly, the newcomer, on the other hand, wears a spotless uniform, signifying her early opposition to the Severance procedure. These minor variations enable the audience to empathize with the characters' emotional journeys and offer a glimpse into their personal challenges.

- *The Strategic Use of Color:*

  The costumes also make strategic use of color. The employees' outfits' muted, neutral colors emphasize how corporate and antiseptic their lives are. But occasionally, there are bursts of more vibrant color, like the red of the Overtime Contingency button or the sporadic splash of color in personal belongings. These colorful moments serve as visual clues that highlight the moment's emotional or narrative significance.

Time-Blurring Aesthetics

Severance's time-blurring aesthetics are among its most distinctive features. The concept of time is a recurring theme in the show, especially in the way the characters perceive their multiple lives. This sense of chronological dislocation is facilitated by the world's visual and stylistic choices, which also produce a sense of bewilderment and discomfort that reflects the characters' psychological experiences.

Timeless Aesthetic Choices

The decor of the workplace and the utilization of costumes and props give the Severance universe a timeless quality. The setting's retro-futuristic vibe gives the impression that it takes place in an indeterminate era when the past, present, and future are all constantly changing. The office's neat, clinical lines give the impression that Lumon exists outside of traditional time, as though it were from the 1970s or the near future.

- *Technology's Ambiguity:*

  Additionally, Severance purposefully uses antiquated technology. Older, seemingly antiquated technology, like the large office phones and archaic computers, coexists with the sophisticated, intrusive severance procedure, creating the impression that time at Lumon Industries is meaningless. The entire sense of confusion and outdatedness that characterizes the show's setting is exacerbated by this lack of technological cohesion.

- *Memory and Temporal Distortion:*

  The way the show depicts the passage of time for its characters is the most remarkable aspect of the time-blurring aesthetics. The "Innies" perceive their professional life as being totally separate from their personal lives as a result of the severance process itself, which causes a fractured sense of time. This sensation of temporal distortion is enhanced by the visual strategies used in the presentation, such as the numerous changes in viewpoint and the repeating of specific motifs. The protagonists' time is always changing, and the series is made more confusing and tense by their inability to balance their personal and professional lives.

Severance's office environment is a blank space where time doesn't pass in a straight line. The characters' emotional and psychological paralysis is reflected in the layout of Lumon Industries' office and wider environment. Their memories are broken, their identities are taken away, and time is turned into a tool that the company uses to control its workers.

Chapter 11: Legacy and Critical Reception

Both critics and viewers have been enthralled by Severance, which has sparked heated debates over its themes, narrative, and innovative performances. The show has earned a position in the canon of must-watch television because of its breathtaking cinematography and its in-depth, provocative examination of identity and corporate power. Like any show that challenges the conventions of storytelling, Severance has received both praise and criticism. Its influence has been felt on many different platforms, and it has won multiple awards and accolades. This chapter will look at Severance's legacy and critical reception, evaluating the praise it has gotten and the responses from both fans and critics.

Reactions From the Audience and Critical Acclaim

Awards and Accolades

Upon its debut, Severance immediately became a critical favorite, receiving accolades for its innovative approach to television, striking visuals, and examination of timely social themes. The show's fusion of suspense, surrealism, and emotional depth captivated both critics and viewers. Consequently, the show garnered a plethora of esteemed accolades and nominations, solidifying its legacy in television history.

- *The Primetime Emmys*

    Being recognized at the 2022 Primetime Emmy Awards was one of the most important turning points in Severance's history. Among its many nominations was Outstanding Drama Series, which is a noteworthy accomplishment for a first season. The show's director, Ben Stiller, was further solidified as a key contributor to its success when he received a nomination for Outstanding Directing for a Drama Series. Additionally, the show was nominated for Outstanding Supporting Actress in a Drama Series for Patricia Clarkson, who plays the cunning Harmony Cobel, and Outstanding Lead Actor in a Drama Series for Adam Scott, whose depiction of Mark Scout was praised for its nuanced complexity. The Emmy Awards recognition demonstrated the show's capacity to differentiate itself in a crowded field of esteemed dramas.

- *The Golden Globes*

  Severance made headlines again at the 2023 Golden Globes, receiving several nominations. A significant achievement that demonstrated the show's powerful influence in the television business was its win for *Best Television Series – Drama*. Adam Scott received *Best Performance by an Actor in a Television Series – Drama* for his portrayal of Mark Scout, which was well praised and demonstrated the character's depth of feeling. By drawing in new audiences and solidifying its position as a television stand out, the Golden Globes assisted in transforming Severance from a niche series into a larger cultural phenomenon.

- *Critics' Choice Awards and Other Recognitions*

Additionally, the series received nominations and wins at the Critics' Choice Awards, where it was honored for its outstanding acting, writing, and directing. Adam Scott received numerous accolades and nominations for his performance as Mark Scout at numerous award shows, such as the

Screen Actors Guild Awards and the Satellite Awards. These honors demonstrated how successfully Severance combined high-concept narrative with incredibly realistic human hardships. The program was also praised for its outstanding production design and its role in advancing television's use of visual storytelling.

Analyzing Reviews from Critics and Fans

Severance has received extremely good reviews from critics and fans alike, who have praised its complexity and ambition. Many viewers have found resonance in the show's examination of themes like memory, identity, corporate domination, and the fuzziness of the boundaries between work and personal life, especially in today's corporate-driven culture. The show has received a lot of praise, but it has also drawn criticism for its slow-burning, intricate plotlines and purposefully vague treatment of some of them. Here, we'll examine the most frequent criticism and fan comments made about the show.

- *Acclaim for Its Unique Concept and Storytelling*

  Severance's uniqueness has been a major source of acclaim. The idea of the show—that employees' memories are "severed" between their personal and professional lives—has received praise for its audacity and capacity to creatively address current challenges. The show has received constant praise from critics for posing important moral queries on corporate dominance, the erasure of individuality, and the effects of technology on contemporary society. The idea of the "Innie" and "Outie" lifestyles' duality captivated viewers' attention and made them consider their own relationships with autonomy and work-life balance.

The tone of the show has also received a lot of attention for its skill at fusing the fantastical with the real, which keeps viewers interested by evoking a sense of discomfort and mystery. Although slow, Severance's pacing is deliberate, enabling the story to develop in a way that heightens the sense of mystery and enhances the satisfaction of the final disclosures. Many critics referred to the episode as a television masterclass because of its unconventional storytelling approaches and well-crafted tension.

- *The Performance of Adam Scott*

One of the most notable performances in Severance has been Adam Scott's portrayal of Mark Scout. Scott's ability to portray the emotional depth and sensitivity of a man dealing with sorrow while navigating the terrifying corporate machinery of Lumon Industries has been praised by both critics and fans. The viewer may relate to Mark's internal conflict because of his nuanced portrayal of a guy divided between his "Innie" and "Outie" sides. Mark is one of the most talked-about aspects of the show because of his portrayal, which strikes a chord with many viewers as both a highly sympathetic character and someone who unwittingly participated in Lumon's control system.

With numerous nominations and wins for Best Actor in a Television Drama, Scott's performance was well-known and highlighted how crucial his character is to the show's emotional heart. His rapport with the ensemble cast also won praise from critics, raising the emotional stakes of the series even higher.

- *The Visual Style and World-Building*

  The flawless world-building of Severance has also been a recurring topic in the compliments. The antiseptic Lumon Industries offices and the strange, retro-futuristic technology are only two examples of the show's striking visual design, which has been praised as a major factor in the series' immersive experience. Critics and fans alike have commented on the creepy, dreamy ambiance that surrounds the series, with its use of muted hues, minimalistic architecture, and great attention to detail. One major area of appreciation for the program has been its ability to visually represent the psychological moods of its characters, particularly in the eerie portrayal of time, memory, and space.

- *Identity and Memory Themes*

  Viewers have responded well to Severance's examination of memory, identity, and self-awareness, especially at a time when the lines separating personal and professional life are becoming increasingly hazy. Its depiction of a corporately controlled society where individuality is given up for efficiency has led critics to compare it to classic dystopian novels like Aldous Huxley's Brave New World and George Orwell's 1984. The show has received recognition for its ability to contextualize these complex philosophical issues in a contemporary, relevant way, transforming it from a thriller into a provocative reflection on human nature.

- *Reactions from Fans and Cult Following:*

Severance has generated a lot of conversation among fans, with people debating and speculating about the show's deeper meanings. Fans may now discuss the show's moral quandaries, analyze the episodes, and post their opinions on social media sites like Reddit and Twitter. The show has developed a devoted following that is keen to delve into every facet of its intricate plot. The ability of the show to evoke a sense of mystery and suspense in viewers is among the most noteworthy features of fan reactions.

A strong fan theory culture has resulted from the doubts Severance aroused over the real nature of Lumon, the identities of its employees, and the ultimate objectives of the severance procedure. Every new season is eagerly anticipated by fans, who analyze every hint to find out what might happen next.

Chapter 12: The Cultural Impact of *Severance*

Severance has unquestionably had a cultural impact since its premiere, serving as a significant contributor to the changing field of contemporary storytelling in addition to being an exciting and thought-provoking work of television. The show has transcended its genre to become a cultural icon because of its inventive story structure, eerie atmosphere, and in-depth examination of subjects like identity, autonomy, and corporate power. Its distinct perspective on memory and the human psyche has generated conjecture, fan theories, and a more in-depth societal discussion on individual rights, technology, and the workplace. Additionally, by introducing novel viewpoints to both the psychological thriller and science fiction genres, Severance has made important contributions to both. In addition to its enduring contributions to science fiction and psychological thriller narrative, this chapter will examine Severance's cultural influence, with a particular emphasis on fan hypotheses and conjectures.

Fan Theories and Speculations

The diverse range of fan ideas and conjectures that Severance has sparked is among its most intriguing features. Because of the series' ambiguous blending of mystery, dystopia, and psychological terror, viewers have been talking about it a lot. In order to express their thoughts and speculations regarding the actual nature of Lumon Industries, the severance process, and the motivations of the show's protagonists, fans have flocked to online forums such as Reddit and Twitter. In addition to building excitement for upcoming episodes, these conversations have given viewers a sense of camaraderie as they try to solve the show's many riddles.

The Severance Procedure's Nature

The severance procedure itself, which divides employees' memories into two separate identities—their "Innie" self, which only exists at work, and their "Outie" self, which is ignorant of the events and activities of their work life—is one of the main mysteries of severance. Regarding the beginnings of this process and its eventual goal, fans have conjectured extensively. Some people think that Lumon Industries is a front for a much bigger and darker organization because of its unsettling and almost cult-like ambiance. According to a popular view, the severance process is a component of a larger social experiment or psychological manipulation rather than just a corporate tool. This idea suggests that the practice might be a part of a larger attempt by the government or corporations to manipulate society by influencing employees' memories in order to increase their compliance or effectiveness.

Some people think that the severance process has a more moral or personal purpose, possibly related to the suffering or loss that certain workers have gone through. For instance, it's evident that Mark Scout is grieving deeply over the loss of his wife, and many fans have theorized that the severance policy was put in place to help workers cope with the hardships of their personal life. But as the show progresses, the distinction between exploitation and compassion becomes more hazy, giving rise to other ideas regarding Lumon Industries' actual intentions and the long-term impacts of severance on the mental and emotional health of its workers.

The Secret of Lumon's and Kier Eagan's History

Another common topic of conjecture concerns Lumon Industries' mysterious founder, Kier Eagan. Although the show suggests that Lumon staff members venerate Eagan with cult-like adoration, not much is revealed about the guy or his genuine motivations. Supporters have conjectured that Eagan might have some firsthand knowledge of the severance technique, possibly having undergone it to deal with a traumatic situation in his own life. Some even think that Eagan's ideas and philosophy are part of a broader ideological movement, possibly one that combines social engineering in a perverse way or commerce with mysticism. Fans have excitedly attempted to figure out Eagan's part in the bigger story, since his presence hovers over the series like a shadow.

Numerous fan ideas have also been stoked by the enigmatic *"severed floor"* and the sinister mysteries of Lumon Industries. According to certain theories, the "severed floor" may provide the secret to the company's operations and the workings of the severance method. Others think it's a covert lab where people who have had their bodies severed are used in trials to examine the procedure's neurological and psychological repercussions. Fans remain interested and invested in learning the truth about Lumon's operations because of the series' feeling of intrigue and the fact that there are still a lot of unanswered questions.

The Real Nature of "Outies" and "Innies"

The relationship between the "*Innie*" and "*Outie*" personas is another major mystery that has captivated people' attention. The lifestyles of "*Innie*" and "*Outie*" may not be as distinct as they appear, according to some fan speculations. According to certain beliefs, the "*Innie*" self's memories may have an impact on the "*Outie*" self's behavior, and vice versa. Significant ethical concerns regarding the nature of consciousness and individual agency are brought up by this blurring of the lines between the two identities. When your memories and behaviors are split up into two separate identities, what does it mean to be in charge of your life? How much freedom do Lumon workers actually have, and will they ever be able to escape the restrictions of the severance process? These inquiries contribute to the intricate and constantly growing mythos of Severance and drive a large portion of the fan discussion surrounding it.

Contributions to the Science Fiction and Psychological Thriller Genres

Severance is frequently classified as a psychological thriller, although its influence goes beyond that subgenre. The show has revitalized the science fiction and psychological thriller genres by fusing aspects of corporate satire, psychological horror, and dystopian fiction. In addition to tackling modern concerns like corporate power, mental health, and the effect of technology on individual freedom, the series questions conventional ideas of reality and identity.

Pushing the Limits of Psychological Thriller

Severance is fundamentally a psychological thriller that explores the depths of the human psyche. The program pushes the limits of vision and reality, making viewers consider what is real and what is made up. By establishing two distinct identities within a single person and laying the groundwork for a thorough investigation of memory, autonomy, and personal freedom, the severance technique itself is a type of psychological manipulation. Severance therefore continues the tradition of psychological thrillers such as Black Mirror and The Twilight Zone, which frequently depict protagonists ensnared in control structures that restrict their perception of both the outside world and themselves.

But Severance's realistic treatment of these difficult subjects is what distinguishes it from other psychological thrillers. Severance exploits its disturbing premise to provoke deeper, more philosophical concerns about the nature of employment, identity, and corporate power, in contrast to many other shows that use psychological manipulation for flimsy thrills or dramatic drama. The program poses significant moral dilemmas about the decisions people make at work and the psychological effects of organizational structures that aim to separate and compartmentalize the human condition. This creative strategy has solidified Severance as a seminal series within the genre.

Intentionally Left Blank

Chapter 13: The Future of *Severance*

Anticipation for the third season of Severance is rising as the show's mind-bending plot and provocative themes continue to enthrall viewers. With its distinctive examination of corporate domination, psychological manipulation, and the meaning of identity, the series has already had a significant impact on television, and viewers are excited to see where the plot will go next. There have been a few teasers, trailers, and interviews that provide hints of what Season Three will be like, even if a lot is still unknown. We will examine what we currently know about Severance Season Three in this chapter, delving into the most recent teasers, fan theories, and Dan Erickson's outlook for the program's future.

Trailers, Teasers, and Speculations

With just a few teasers and videos teasing the upcoming season, Severance has so far mainly kept its intentions for Season Three a secret. In order to preserve the show's distinctive tension and keep viewers on edge, the makers have been cautious not to give away too much. But the brief looks provided by early promotional materials and behind-the-scenes videos have been sufficient to generate a plethora of conjecture and ideas regarding potential future developments.

The Key Characters' Return

The destiny of the characters following the dramatic Season Two conclusion is one of the most important topics for viewers. There are a lot of unanswered questions at the end of Season Two, especially in relation to what will happen to Mark Scout (played by Adam Scott), Helly Riggs (Britt Lower), Dylan (Zach Cherry), and Irving (John Turturro).

At the end of the episode, a number of people start to rebel against the repressive corporate structure that has dominated their lives, hinting at profound changes within Lumon Industries. Viewers are excited to see how these issues will be explored in Season Three after the Season Two finale hinted at the possibility of the characters' worlds clashing in ever-more-dangerous ways.

Although Mark, Helly, and the other important characters appear briefly in the early teasers, not much is known about their future plans. One of the main topics of fan discussion is whether the severance process will be reversed or if the characters will keep attempting to escape Lumon.

As they begin to face the emotional, psychological, and personal costs of the severance procedure, some fans have conjectured that Season Three would examine the idea of characters learning to blend their "Innie" and "Outie" personas.

Will the show concentrate on the fallout from this disclosure, or will it turn its attention to the more extensive plots involving Lumon and its actual intent? Many fan ideas concerning the characters' and the company's futures have emerged as a result of these issues, which have dominated most of the internet discussion.

The Darker Agenda of Lumon Industries

The increasing sense of danger surrounding Lumon Industries is another important feature hinted at in early advertising materials. The world of the show was extended beyond the company's headquarters in Season Two, which also provided additional insight into the mystery forces at work behind the scenes and the mysterious founder Kier Eagan. An unsettling remark regarding the company's actual motivations is introduced in the season finale, raising the possibility of a wider conspiracy with potentially worldwide repercussions.

Fans have conjectured that Season Three would explore Lumon Industries' beginnings in greater detail, especially the enigmatic "severed floor" and how it relates to Kier Eagan's vision. According to some beliefs, Lumon's influence might go beyond the severance-affected employees; it might even have a wider ideological agenda or control over other facets of society. Fans have been able to piece together hints from the show's slow burn, and many think that Season Three will reveal Lumon's entire strength.

New Locations and World Expansion

The idea that the Severance universe will grow is a recurrent element in the teasers and trailers for Season Three. We saw more of the corporate hierarchy, the psychological effects of severance on workers, and the larger conspiracy around Lumon in Season Two, which took us outside of the office. Excitement over what might be discovered has been raised by the notion that Season Three will unveil more of the globe.

Season Three is expected to feature a significant number of new locations, according to rumors and conjecture. As Mark and the other characters leave Lumon's borders, will we get a better look at the outside world? Will Lumon-related places or new corporate settings be investigated? As they start to solve the mystery of the severance procedure, viewers are excited to watch how the narrative expands and how the worlds of the characters may change.

Dan Erickson's Vision for the Continuation

One thing is certain, even though a lot of the plot is still unknown: Dan Erickson, the creator of Severance, has a definite idea for how the series will go forward. From the start, Erickson has created a world that combines dark satire, psychological suspense, and science fiction while tackling issues that appeal to modern audiences, like the conflict between institutional control and individual liberty, the impact of technology on human lives, and the dehumanizing effects of corporate culture.

Developing Identity and Memory Themes

In Season Three, Erickson has made it clear that he wants to continue examining the main themes of memory and identity. The severance process itself serves as a metaphor for how people divide themselves into personal and professional spheres, compartmentalizing various facets of their lives. According to Erickson's interviews, Season Three will go more into the effects of this identity fragmentation and the possibility that characters will regain their independence and reconnect their *"Innie"* and *"Outie"* identities.

One of the main topics of the series is this investigation of memory and identity, and Erickson has alluded to the fact that the third season of the program will further test viewers' comprehension of these ideas. Will the characters grow more firmly rooted in their own realities or will they manage to reconcile their internal conflicts? The story will continue to focus heavily on the psychological effects of the severance process, with Erickson promising a more thorough examination of the mental and emotional toll it has on Lumon Industries' workers.

The Morality of Corporate Power and Control

The ethics of corporate power and the manner in which organizations can influence people for their own benefit are other topics that Erickson has indicated a wish to delve deeper into in Season Three. Fans have conjectured that Season Three will disclose even more about Lumon

Industries' actual mission, as Season Two had unveiled additional facets of the company's evil activities. Erickson has talked about his fascination in the series' ethical issues, such as the price of advancement, how corporate power shapes people's lives, and what freedom means in a society where technology and surveillance are taking over.

The conflict between individual liberty and institutional authority has never been more evident than with the disclosures of Season Two. This issue will probably be further developed in Erickson's third season vision, which will examine the repercussions of operating in a system where the boundaries between work and personal life are purposefully blurred and dissent can have disastrous effects.

The Characters' Development

According to Erickson, Season Three will not hold back when it comes to the characters' emotional and psychological development, especially that of the main cast of Lumon employees. Characters like Mark, Helly, Dylan, and Irving have undergone significant change as a result of the events of Seasons One and Two, and Erickson has hinted that these characters' paths may continue to take unforeseen turns. He has hinted in interviews that the characters would start to make decisions that directly oppose the system in which they have been imprisoned and rebel against Lumon Industries' repressive powers.

According to Erickson, the characters' journeys will always be rooted in their own hardships, making their moral decisions and emotional development just as significant as the greater plot. The tension between corporate control and individual agency will intensify as the show progresses, and the characters will have to face their own reasons and beliefs as they deal with the fallout from their choices.

Conclusion: *Severance* – A Tale of Two Lives

Severance's complex examination of memory, identity, and the dehumanizing effects of corporate power keeps viewers enthralled as it progresses through its seasons. The series is fundamentally a tale of duality—of broken lives, secrets, and the ongoing struggle between individual freedom and governmental authority. A brilliant creative team and a remarkable ensemble cast have developed the ground-breaking story, which has enthralled audiences and sparked discussions about the price of progress, the morality of contemporary workplace culture, and the human desire for connection and self-awareness.

Reflecting on the Journey of the Series

From the beginning, *Severance* presented a novel idea: a business that splits workers' memories, forming two separate identities in each individual—one for the workplace and one for their personal lives. This audacious idea swiftly emerged as the main inspiration for the series, providing a fresh perspective on the intricacies of contemporary life. Viewers are eager to learn the truth about Lumon Industries and its deceptive tactics because of the show's deft blending of mystery, psychological horror, and dark satire.

We observe as the lives of characters like Dylan, Helly Riggs, and Mark Scout start to fall apart in unexpected ways. The story gradually transforms from what begins as an apparently straightforward office-based dystopia into a fascinating examination of the human condition, examining how people can get consumed by the demands of their employers and the effects of contemporary systems on mental and emotional health. Grief, resistance, ambition, and the search for truth are all aspects of the human experience that are represented by the journeys of each character.

One of the most remarkable aspects of the series has been its transformation from a small-scale, intimate tale of identities that have been severed to a more comprehensive investigation of institutional corruption. The stakes have increased with each season, providing new insights into Lumon Industries' world and the individuals entangled in its webs. *Severance* compels us to consider our own lives and the structures that influence them through its erratic story turns and intense scenes. *Do invisible boundaries keep us from fully comprehending ourselves and others, causing us to live severed lives as well?*

Fundamentally, *Severance* is still a profoundly philosophical series that examines issues of autonomy, identity, and the price of living in a world that is becoming more and more divided. The show challenges us to consider the moral ramifications of the corporate world's control over our time, ideas, and behavior as well as the very essence of employment and the cost of maintaining our standard of living.

Final Thoughts on Identity and Duality

It is impossible to overlook *Severance's* primary theme of duality. Dualities that many people encounter in their personal lives are reflected in the idea of having two separate lives—one for work and one for home. We all put on masks, changing our actions to suit various social or professional settings. Occasionally, these masks become so ingrained that it is hard to tell the difference between who we are and who we believe we should be.

The idea of the "*Innie*" and "*Outie*"—the separated selves of each employee—is the most obvious example of this dualism. While the "*Outie*" leads a different life outside of the workplace and is ignorant of the happenings of the workday, the "*Innie*" only exists within the boundaries of Lumon Industries and is responsible for meeting the needs of the firm. As the protagonists' disparate lives become more and more cut off from one another, this produces a strong feeling of alienation. Some people experience a severe existential crisis as a result of the difference between these selves becoming intolerable.

This dualism is especially noticeable for the main character, Mark Scout. The emotional toll of leading a divided life is highlighted by his attempt to balance his own anguish with his responsibilities as the leader of the fired staff. Mark's journey turns into one of self-discovery and defiance against a system that aims to eradicate uniqueness as he starts to doubt the meaning of his employment and the rationale behind his choice to go through the severance procedure.

As the aggressive newbie, Helly Riggs represents yet another type of duality: her concealed fragility beneath her strong demeanor and her disobedience of the system. The human experience of struggling with one's own identity and purpose in the face of enormous external forces is reflected in her effort to regain her autonomy and face the truth of her circumstances.

In the end, *Severance* is a meditation on the notion that identity is fluid rather than fixed, influenced by our decisions and the forces in our environment. *What happens when you lose touch with who you are?* is the question posed by the show. And how much does the appearance of control cost you?

The show also addresses the broader discussion about corporate deception, workplace culture, and technology. Many people in today's society suffer from psychological severance, which is a disconnection between their personal and professional lives that is made worse by the increase in digital surveillance, remote work, and the need to be "on" all the time for employers. These fears are tapped into by severance, which pushes individuals to their breaking point. The show explores what may occur if corporations were to completely take over a person's psyche, wiping out all memories of the individual and treating employees like insignificant parts of a larger system.

In summary, *Severance* is more than just a thriller; it is a study of the human condition and a somber depiction of a society where it is becoming harder to distinguish between one's personal and professional lives. Viewers are encouraged to consider their own experiences of leading divided lives as a result of the characters' duality, which speaks to the larger issue of identity fragmentation. Severance will undoubtedly continue to question our ideas of memory, free will, and corporate power as the series progresses, ultimately serving as a warning about the perils of losing oneself in the name of production and profit. Ultimately, Severance compels us to ask: *How can we define ourselves when the boundaries between our actual selves and our ideal selves are so dangerously blurred?*

Printed in Dunstable, United Kingdom